Fundamental

Jon Lurie, Jimmy Clarke, and the
following athletes were photographed
for this book:
   Janine Avent,
   Amy Campion,
   Dan Dhruva,
   Dylan Farr,
   Clark Hurlbut,
   Bruce Mullinax,
   Leslee Olson,
   Trevor Phillips,
   Sabrina Sadeghi,
   Casey Savage,
   Forrest Wieland.

Fundamental

SNOWBOARDING

Jon Lurie

Photographs by Jimmy Clarke

Lerner Publications Company ● Minneapolis

For Jane and our girls, Tony Rios,
and Freedom

Library of Congress Cataloging-in-Publication Data

Lurie, Jon.
    Fundamental snowboarding/Jon Lurie ; photographs by Jimmy Clarke.
        p. cm. — (Fundamental Sports)
    Includes bibliographical references and index.
    Summary: introduces the history and techniques of snowboarding.
        ISBN 0–8225–3457–6 (alk. paper)
        1. Snowboarding—Juvenile literature. [1. Snowboarding.]
    I. Title.
GV857.S57L87   1996
796.9—dc20   95–11721

Manufactured in the United States of America

1 2 3 4 5 6 HP 01 00 99 98 97 96

The Fundamental Sports series was conceptualized by editor Julie Jensen, designed by graphic artist Michael Tacheny, and composed on a Macintosh computer by Robert Mauzy.

Photo Acknowledgments
Photographs reproduced with the permission of: pp. 8, 38, 59, ALLSPORT/Mike Powell; pp. 9, 10, 15 (all), 18, 19, 21, 58, 63, Burton Snowboards; p. 11, Courtesy of Tom Sims; pp. 40, 61, Courtesy of Chris Thorson; pp. 51, 53 (top right), Photo by Mark Gallup.

All diagrams by Laura Westlund.

Contents

Chapter 1

How This Sport Got Started

Imagine a sport that combines the beauty of surfing, the high-speed thrill of downhill skiing, the punk styles of skateboarding, and the grace of ballet. That sport is snowboarding.

Standing sideways on a smooth, wooden board, snowboarders glide down mountain slopes at speeds up to 65 miles per hour. They spray snow like frozen rainbows, 30 feet into the air. They daringly fly off cliffs, settling into soft, white snow far below. They dance on hard-packed snow, twisting and leaping, always thinking of new tricks for the next run!

Color-Coded Snow

Ski area operators designate their runs as easy, intermediate, or difficult to help skiers and snowboarders choose the runs on which they want to ski or snowboard.

A green circle indicates a run for beginners and inexperienced skiers and snowboarders. Green runs are often wide and not very steep. Green runs are great for learning how to snowboard and for warming up at the start of an outing. Remember, there often are many beginners on green runs, and they aren't always skiing or snowboarding under control. Watch out for human missiles flying down the run!

A blue square signals an intermediate run. Of course, one person's definition of intermediate may not match another's. Some blue runs have moguls; others are steep with sharp twists. Be prepared to stretch yourself when you decide to ride a blue run. Often blue runs will have easy stretches so you can catch your breath or regroup after the more difficult parts.

A black diamond means excitement. Black diamond runs are designed for experts and advanced skiers and snowboarders. Black diamonds are steep and often narrow. Most black diamonds have moguls or crests. Black diamond runs are often bordered by trees and steep ditches.

It's always fun to challenge yourself, but be smart. Snowboard on runs you can handle. Stay healthy and in one piece by watching out for others on the runs.

Before snowboarding became widely recognized, children stood on sleds and imitated surfers. It isn't surprising that surfers, in search of ways to create an endless summer, were some of the first to design and ride "snow surfboards." Many of these early boards were little more than sanded planks held to the rider's feet with ropes or nothing at all.

Skateboarders were also eager to find a way to take their sport to the top of snowy mountains. After removing the wheels from the bottoms of their skateboards, they bolted the tops to polyethylene molds and tried to ride them down the hills.

Most of these early designs weren't very successful. Some boards slid on the snow but were difficult to control. Smaller models, fashioned after skateboards, sunk instantly into any surface softer than ice.

While known attempts to surf on snow date back to the 1920s, it wasn't until 1965 that the modern snowboarding movement began. That year, Sherman Poppen invented the Snurfer for his children by bolting two skis together. A rider held a rope attached to the Snurfer's nose (front section) for stability.

Snowboards with names like "Winterstick" and "Skiboard" first appeared in toy shops, discount stores, and comic book ads in the mid-1970s. These boards, made of hard plastic, were an improvement over many homemade devices. Plastic reduced the friction between the board and the snow, allowing riders to go faster than before.

These upgraded snowboards still didn't have reliable **bindings**. This meant that riders whizzed down the mountain at even higher speeds, but with even less control than on earlier boards. Many twisted ankles and broken legs resulted.

In the early 1970s, Jake Burton began a series of experiments that would eventually earn him the title "Godfather of Snowboarding." These experiments would change what had been known as "snowsurfing" and make "snowboarding" a sport in its own right.

Jake, a skier and surfer, had been modifying and riding Snurfers since he was in high school. Jake was frustrated by the creeping pace of change at American ski resorts where snowboarders weren't allowed to ride chairlifts. Chairlifts are machines that take people up a mountain. There were resort owners who feared that snowboards were uncontrollable. They worried that the new sport would attract "the wrong clientele."

Since he wasn't allowed to ride the chairlifts, Jake tied his latest snowboard to his back and hiked up the slopes of Stratton Mountain, Vermont, after the resort was closed. Once on top, he strapped the board to his boots and carved his way down. With each run, he learned more about snowboard design. He learned that quality snowboard design had less to do with surfing and skateboarding and more to do with downhill skiing. He decided that wood, not plastic, was the best material for the top, or deck, of the snowboard. Plastic got too hard on cold days. For a rider to have control, the snowboard would have to be flexible in all conditions. Squared edges were necessary, but they weren't enough.

Jake Burton began snowboarding while in high school. Later, he researched and designed snowboards and created a company to manufacture them.

Like downhill skis, snowboards must have smooth, sharp, metal edges to allow for quick stops and control in icy conditions. Plastic was still necessary to reduce friction, so Jake borrowed from skiing a tough, flexible plastic called P-tex, which he applied to the bottom of his wooden decks.

The length and width were also serious considerations. Jake discovered that long surf-type boards could be turned sharply at high speeds but not on **hardpack**—crusty, icy snow. He also found that shorter boards made quick movements easier. To accommodate a wide variety of maneuvers, he settled

on a board that was longer than a skateboard and shorter than a surfboard. After years of hikes up the mountain and long hours in his workshop, he created a snowboard that was fast, easy to maneuver in a wide range of conditions, safe, and inexpensive to make. Best of all, his snowboards could do everything skis could do—and more!

Jake's new boards weren't taken seriously at first. Most ski shop owners refused to sell them, calling them dangerous toys. Jake managed to convince a few retailers that snowboarding was a serious sport. On the American coasts, where surfing had long been popular, snowboarding took off. Other snowboarders started their own snowboard companies, imitating the designs Jake had created. The snowboard makers added new features and improved old ones. Riders soon had dozens of models from which to choose.

Jake Burton was just one of many snowboarding pioneers. Tom Sims built the first known snowboard in a high school shop class in 1963. Dimitrije Molovich created Winterstick snowboards in 1975. But without effective bindings, Wintersticks were practical only in deep snow conditions. Without the solid support of bindings, snowboarders didn't have control and injuries continued to be a problem.

In 1983 a rider named Jeff Grell made a binding system that was effective in all snow conditions. Grell's binding surrounded the snowboarder's foot with a hard plastic shell. The shell was clamped tightly to the board with straps and metal buckles. With these bindings, riders could maintain control even on hardpack, which is the kind of snow found at most ski resorts.

Thousands of riders wanted to be allowed on ski lifts. European resort owners realized that snowboarding would pump more money into their business, but many American resort owners needed convincing. In the late 1980s, the United States went into a recession. Fewer skiers could afford lift tickets. Many resorts went out of business. Most of the resorts that survived into the 1990s did so because they opened their lifts to snowboarders. By the mid-1980s, between 80 and 90 percent of the ski areas in North America allowed snowboarding.

There are now snowboarders in at

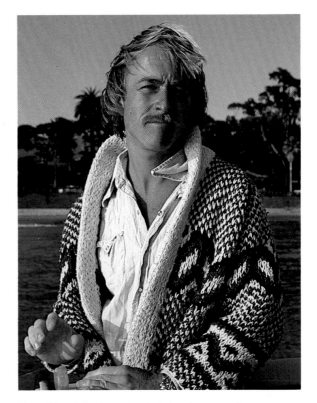

Tom Sims' high school shop class project was building a snowboard. He has continued to develop snowboards for the last 30 years.

least 75 nations and on 5 continents, which qualifies snowboarding for Olympic Games status. If the International Olympic Committee approves it, snowboarding will be contested in the 2002 Winter Games.

Snowboarding technology, styles, and techniques have come far since the days of snurfing. Still, the basic pleasure of cruising sideways down a mountain slope on a single, smooth board remains unchanged.

Chapter 2

BASICS

Equipment

The first step in learning how to snowboard is unavoidably the same for everyone: get your hands on a snowboard. Because a new board costs several hundred dollars, most people borrow one from another rider or rent one at the mountain for their first time. Used snowboards can be bought at a great discount. They're usually available at preseason ski-swaps and snowboarding specialty shops.

Whether you're buying a snowboard or deciding which type to rent for the day, choose a board that's right for what you intend to do with it. To decide what your style will be, think of other activities you've done. Skateboarders, for instance, may recall that what they enjoy about skateboarding is doing 360-degree turns and flying off a curb.

The Snowboard

This diagram of a snowboard shows its parts and explains their uses:

Nose: The front, or leading, end of the snowboard. Rounded, upturned shape reduces friction by pushing snow under, rather than over, the board. Also called the shovel.

Heelside edge: The edge on the same side as the snowboarder's heels. For carving backside turns, down-mountain stopping and traversing.

Bindings: Fasteners that hold the snowboarder's feet onto the snowboard. **Mounting Sockets** (not shown): The drill holes that hold the bindings to the snowboard with screws.

Leash: Fastens around rider's leg to prevent runaway snowboards.

Stomp Pad: Provides friction for rear foot when riding out of back binding.

Toeside edge: The edge on the same side as the snowboarder's toes. For carving frontside turns, up-mountain stopping and traversing.

Tail: The rear, or trailing, end of the snowboard. A board with a shovel tail may be ridden either direction.

Freestyle snowboard

A **freestyle** snowboard is short and flexible. It has a **shovel** on both ends and low-backed bindings. With a freestyle snowboard, you can duplicate your skateboarding tricks on the snow. If you want to carve at high speed or ride in snow up to your neck, choose an **alpine** design board. This board will be long, narrow, and stiff. An alpine board has high-backed bindings and a squared or **asymmetrical** tail.

The size of snowboard you'll need depends on your height, weight, and the length of your feet. Because you stand sideways on a snowboard, the board should be about as wide as your feet are long. That way, your toes and heels won't dig in during turns. People with exceptionally long feet may want to use exceptionally wide boards. Children and short adults use smaller snowboards than taller riders. Boards vary in length from about 4 feet to almost 6 feet. A snowboard's flexibility, or **flex,** is as important as its length. The heavier the rider, the stiffer the board needs to be.

Alpine snowboard

Snowboard Art

A snowboard's artwork can reflect the personality of its rider. Snowboard manufacturers employ teams of artists to create drawings, paintings, and photographs that express their feelings about riding. Sometimes these works are one-of-a-kind originals. Other times they are mass-produced. Many snowboarders prefer to design their own artwork. The variety and ingenuity of snowboard imagery contributes greatly to the sense of the sport as fresh and modern.

In 1990 Morrow Snowboards commissioned Scott Clum, a former pro rider, to create graphics displays. Clum has inspired many gifted young artists to use the snowboard as a launch pad of self-expression. Professional snowboard artists often spend much of their time riding with company team members. They get their inspiration from the mountain.

In any snowboard shop, you will find the impressive results of these efforts. Some snowboard designs are so eye-catching that you may be tempted to choose a board for what it looks like, rather than for what it can do. While attraction to a sketch, graphic, or painting shouldn't be the primary consideration in the purchase of a snowboard, it is undoubtedly the top tiebreaker.

You also must decide which foot will be your lead foot. If you don't feel a natural tendency to put one foot ahead of the other, think of physical activities you've done in the past. When you held a baseball bat, which foot was closest to the pitcher? That's probably the foot you want in the forward binding.

Snowboarders call a stance in which the rider's right foot is forward a **goofy** stance. A stance in which the snow-boarder's left foot is forward is called a **regular** stance.

At any snowboard shop, you'll find an amazing variety of colors, shapes, and sizes, making your decision both enjoyable and confusing. Whether you're renting or buying, consult a professional snowboarding instructor or an experienced rider to help you choose which type of snowboard and what kind of boots are right for you.

Goofy stance **Regular stance**

Clothing

Standing on frozen, windblown peaks; making turns through face-stinging sleet; riding chairlifts at temperatures below zero—these are the extreme conditions against which snowboarders must protect themselves. Three-level layering is the key to staying warm and dry on the cold and wet slopes.

Materials that breathe (let body moisture out) are used in each layer to prevent soaking sweats. In temperatures below 32 degrees, sweat will freeze to the skin during any period of inactivity, such as riding the chairlift. Here are some recommendations for your layers.

Layer one: Thermal tops and bottoms made of a wool-and-cotton blend or synthetic fabrics such as polypropylene. These blends retain body heat even when they're wet.

Layer two: Lightweight wool or a similar synthetic sweater and pants. Don't wear cotton. Although it's lightweight and comfortable, cotton loses its insulating quality when wet.

Layer three: Water-resistant snowpants and jacket, lined for warmth and made of durable, non-bulky materials such as Cordura, Polar Fleece, or treated denim. Riders often wear long jackets, sometimes to their knees, to keep snow out of their pants.

The most important clothing choices snowboarders make may seem to be trivial items: socks, footwear, and gloves. If you become chilled on the hill, however, the first body parts to be frostbitten will be your fingers and toes. Most riders wear two pairs of wool or wool-and-cotton blend socks.

Snowboarding mittens and gloves are designed with an extended collar and drawstring to seal out the snow. In cold weather, gloved fingers freeze faster than fingers in mittens. Since 90 percent of your body heat is lost through your head, keep a wool hat handy. The old woodsman's saying holds true for snowboarding: *If your fingers or toes get cold, put on a hat.*

One of the great advantages of snowboarding over skiing is the freedom to ride in common, outdoor boots. Riders can hike mountains and fly down the **powder** without first changing into hard-shell boots, as skiers must. Boots specially designed for snowboarding are the first choice of many riders. Snowboarding boots add additional ankle support. Boots, when stuffed with feet and socks, should be snug around heels and ankles. A snug fit helps prevent blisters. A loose-fitting boot decreases your control and increases the chance of injuring your ankles and knees. Don't tie your boots too tightly, however. Boots tied too tightly can cause numb feet and frozen toes. Advanced riders often wear softer, low-cut boots that permit more movement than rigid footwear.

The amazing moves snowboarders make require clear vision. Riding at high speeds can cause tears and blurry vision. Ice pellets or snow can sting your eyes and force them shut. Wear goggles to prevent these problems. Tinted goggles or sunglasses on sunny days can help you see the terrain better.

When getting dressed for snowboarding, keep this in mind: If you're warm

A snowboarding boot is similar to a regular winter boot.

when you begin, you'll soon be hot. When you get hot, you can shed a layer. At sundown, when it starts getting cold, you can add a layer. It's better to be overdressed because you can't add a layer you don't have.

Snowboarding doesn't have to be expensive. If you don't own everything you need to protect yourself in minus-30 windchill conditions, wait until the weather improves. Also, take advantage of fresh snowfalls for your first few outings. Hardpack and ice are difficult surfaces on which to learn. If brush, grass, or rocks are visible, put off snowboarding until after the next big storm. A deep base of snow covered by 6 to 12 inches of new snow makes for ideal learning conditions and creates a soft cushion for you when you fall.

Where to Begin

Although snowboarders are welcome at most ski areas, there are some good reasons not to go to a resort for your debut. You can snowboard on small hills or slopes on public lands for free. On these hills, you can enjoy fresh snow and you won't have to worry about running into other riders and skiers. Hiking up the hills is a good way to warm up your muscles.

Commercial resorts do, however, offer many advantages. Ski areas have a

variety of runs, from simple beginner trails to steep inclines for the experts. Most ski areas have snowboards and boots available for rent. They often have instructors from whom you can take a lesson. Most resorts also make artificial snow, so you won't have to wait for nature to provide perfect conditions. With a chairlift to take you to the top, you will be able to enjoy many runs in a day. The more runs you make, the faster you will improve.

Strapping In

To get started, you have to get your feet strapped onto your snowboard. Sit in the snow with your board below you and parallel to the bottom of the hill. Put your front foot binding on first. Make sure to remove any snow or ice that may have gotten in the bindings. As you ride, any snow remaining in the bindings will pack under your heels. This packed snow will change the shape of the binding, and it won't perform the way it was designed to perform. Tighten the fasteners as firmly as you can without causing discomfort.

You may feel the need to adjust the position of your feet as you stand on the board. Unlike skateboarders, who are free to move their feet, snowboarders must decide on one stance that works for everything they want to do. Most bindings can be adjusted by just loosening and tightening a few screws. Begin with your feet slightly forward of perpendicular to the frontside edge. Does that feel comfortable? If not, adjust the bindings. It may take three or four runs before you discover the position that's right for you.

Now that you're dressed to ride and have a board strapped to your feet, it's time to find your balance limits. Assume a basic athletic stance: knees bent, weight distributed equally on both legs, shoulders facing forward. Lean over the nose of the board. Lean over the back. Then rock onto your toe edge and onto your heel edge. If you fall at this point, you're doing it right. The limits of balance are very small when you aren't moving. As your speed increases, you will be able to lean farther away from the snowboard. At high speeds, you may even be able to touch your cheek to the snow!

Chapter 3

MANEUVERS

A beginner seeing another rider flowing effortlessly down the mountain thinks either, "I could do that—it looks easy," or "I'll never be able to do that—it's impossible." A good rider makes difficult maneuvers look easy. But even the wildest tricks are only a combination of five simple moves.

The point of learning these five basic moves is to be able to ride on a variety of runs and make smooth, easy turns at any speed. Everything else in snowboarding flows from these basics. These five maneuvers can be mastered in a short time. First, however, you must learn how to fall without hurting yourself.

Controlled Fall

Approach snowboarding with the un-derstanding that you will fall many times. Falling is a part of learning. A saying among instructors holds true for nearly every beginner: *You must fall one hundred times before the gods of snowboarding will give you the secret.*

Learning to snowboard doesn't have to be painful. Whenever you feel un-comfortable with your speed, get as low to the ground as possible, face uphill, and reach for the snow with your hands. Let yourself fall gradually onto the uphill side while pushing an edge of the board into the snow to help slow you down.

Leslee is demonstrating a controlled fall. The controlled fall is the best technique for preventing injury. On ice or hardpack, consider wearing elbow pads, knee pads, and a helmet for extra protection.

Quick Fixes to Common Problems

I can't ride forward without the rear end of the snowboard sliding out.

Whichever end of the snowboard has more weight on it will be the end that goes downhill first. Shift your weight over the nose of the snowboard by bending at the waist and dangling your arms ahead of the front binding.

I can't stand on the board. I feel completely out of control.

If you just can't stand on your snowboard without falling immediately, try riding from a crouched position. Many new riders succeed in a crouch because their center of gravity is closer to the ground. Also, if you must fall to stop, you have less distance to travel before you hit the snow.

I can turn, but when I try to go back the other way, my board keeps going. I end up facing backward.

To reverse the direction of a turn, lean your weight on your front foot. Now your back foot can lift off the snow and push the snowboard the other way. Unlike a car, in which the front wheels do the guiding, the snowboard is steered with the rear foot.

Keep in mind that although both feet are tied to the same board, they act independently. Beginners are often reluctant to lean forward for fear of going too fast. But the front edge of the board has to slide down the slope in order to slow down again on the other edge. In other words, when making turns for speed control, you have to speed up before you can slow down.

When done well, the turn is made quickly enough that any speedup is undetectable. Always look in the direction you want to turn.

I usually ski with poles. What do I do with my hands when snowboarding?

In snowboarding, the rider's arms are used for balance and control, much as they are in skiing. Keep your arms loose and ready to react to any changes in equilibrium. There is no right or wrong place to hold the arms. To start, try holding your fists at your chest, like a boxer preparing to fight.

Stop

The first step in learning to ride is learning how to stop without falling. Going back and forth across the hill is one way to stop. But you may not always have the wide expanse of trail and the 5 or 10 seconds this method takes. If, for example, you cruise over a crest and see a downed skier in your path, you must stop quickly to avoid an accident. A rider using the technique Amy is demonstrating can safely stop within a few feet.

Amy twists at her waist to focus her eyes in the direction her board will point at the end of the stop. Shifting her weight to her front foot frees Amy's rear foot to kick the snowboard around.

Amy leans uphill—opposite the direction she's going—for a **backside** stop. As she slows, Amy gradually rocks back over the top of her board while redistributing her weight equally onto both legs.

Sideslip

Riding sideways down the slope is called doing a **sideslip,** or sideslipping. A snowboarder can sideslip on the toeside or the heelside edge. Sabrina is demonstrating a toeside sideslip.

Standing sideways to the run on her toe edge, Sabrina pivots her ankles toward her heels and straightens her legs slightly. She feels for the sweet spot, which is the center point where neither edge catches the snow. As her toe edge comes out of the snow, the board begins to glide. Sabrina constantly adjusts the pivot position of her feet to changes in the terrain. She's careful to keep her heelside edge above the snow. If she doesn't do this, she will end facedown in the snow. When Sabrina wants to stop, she pivots back onto her toes.

Traverse

When riders need to go across a hill, they use the **traverse**. Sabrina keeps in mind that the end of the snowboard that bears the most weight is the end that will go down the hill fastest. If Sabrina puts too much pressure on her rear foot, she may soon go backwards.

Sabrina balances over the uphill edge and shifts her weight slightly to her front foot. She keeps the uphill edge down to keep herself moving crosswise. Sabrina takes care not to dig the downhill edge into the snow because that would send her sliding down the mountain on her back.

Skid

Many times, a rider may want to slow down while continuing on a straight course down the slope. For example, if Trevor sees a **launch** or jump ahead and he's not sure of the terrain on the other side, he goes into a **skid**. Trevor shifts his weight forward and kicks out the tail of his board. He lowers his body to improve his balance. Using moderate pressure on his toe edge, Trevor

slows his snowboard by leaning uphill for a **frontside** skid.

When Trevor reaches the desired speed, he releases the pressure from his toe edge and resumes a normal riding stance. The skid can also be a method of turning. By putting pressure on the uphill edge and alternating heel edge and toe edge, Trevor can make a series of skidding turns.

Riding a Chairlift

One of the first experiences new snowboarders have is riding a chairlift. Injuries caused by falling from chairlifts are rare, but beginners may have some difficulty getting on and off the lift.

All chairlifts have instructional signs to read while you're waiting in line. Snowboarders are required to have their rear foot out of the binding before getting on the lift. They must keep their rear foot loose until they are clear of the lift at the top. Riders are not allowed on chairlifts unless they have a **leash** attached to the front binding and fastened around their leg.

If you have never ridden a chairlift, tell the operator that before it's your turn. Often, the operator will slow the chair or take you by the arm for extra support. When the riders in front of you have left the ground, skate forward to the load line. Look over your shoulder for the chair. The lift operator will catch the chair to make it easier for you to sit down. Grab hold of the chair and sit.

On the way up the mountain, sit back on the chair and lower the safety bar, if there is one. On the way up the mountain, watch other riders. It's one of the best ways to learn.

As you approach the peak, more signs will advise you how to get off the lift. There will be a mound of snow (6 to 10 feet high) at the top. With your front foot, point the nose of the snowboard toward the sky. Slide your rear foot solidly against the rear binding on the **stomp pad**. Let your board glide naturally onto the mound. When the bottom of your snowboard rests entirely on the snow, stand up. Push away from the chair and ride the slope. If you fall, scramble away from the unloading area as quickly as possible to avoid being hit by the next chair.

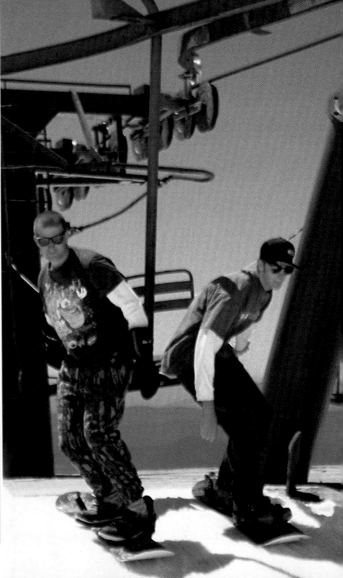

Carve

When a **carve** is done right, the rider feels as if the board is turning itself. The carve leaves a razor-thin track in the snow rather than the wide, snake-like trail imprinted by a skid.

Like a bike racer on a steep track, the rider must ride fast in order to ride high on the edge. Jimmy rocks his weight over the front of the board and presses his heel edge into the snow. He balances all his weight against the momentum of the board, cutting a sharp groove.

Dylan is doing a toeside carve. He shifts his weight forward and presses his toe edge into the snow. He leans with all of his weight against gravity. Riders sometimes describe the rocking motion in a series of carving turns as "totally relaxing" and "hypnotic."

Going Flat Out

Snowboarders sometimes need to travel across flat areas, for example, when they are in the lift line. The motion snowboarders use is called **skating,** but it's not like ice skating. The snowboarders' skating is like skateboarding.

For many people, skating is the most awkward feeling they'll have on a snowboard. The board seems to have a mind of its own, going where it wants, making the rider's front ankle twist in ways previously thought impossible.

To skate effectively, take your rear foot from the binding. Place your weight directly over your front foot by bending your front knee. Lift your rear foot as if you were taking a normal step and pull the board forward.

Small steps make it possible to get your foot back under you quickly. Then you're less apt to lose your balance.

When you have taken three or four consecutive pulls, you may have enough momentum to ride a short distance. Place your rear foot on the stomp pad and glide.

Chapter 4

COMPETITIVE SNOWBOARDING

Snowboarding competitions have progressed from the days when Jake Burton raced for $250 in prize money at the 1979 Snurfer contest. By the middle 1990s, the 3-continent, 33-country professional circuit was awarding more than a million dollars.

When riders gather to compete, they may enter either freestyle or race contests, or both. There are two freestyle events, **halfpipe** and **slopestyle**. The race events are **slalom, parallel slalom, giant slalom,** and **super G**.

The **International Snowboard Federation** sanctions most international, professional contests. The **United States Amateur Snowboard Association (US-ASA)** runs amateur competitions in the United States. Participants are divided into groups according to age. The Menehunes (boys and girls 12 years old and younger) compete in one category. All the other groups are divided by sex and age. The other USASA age groups are: J3 (13- and 14-year-olds), J2 (15 to 16), J1 (17 to 18), Seniors (19 to 25), Masters (26 to 35), Legends (36 to 49), and Methuselahs (50 and older).

Freestyle Competition

● *Halfpipe*

The halfpipe is a channel, 250 to 350 feet long, dug into the snow on a gradual slope. Its walls rise 7 to 14 feet on either side. Riders glide down the incline, gaining speed, and then hurl themselves up the smooth walls and into the air. This is called **catching air**. While in the air, the riders perform tricks. They land back on the wall and glide up the opposite side.

A rider will catch 5 to 10 airs during an average routine. The tricks are performed 3 to 10 feet above the roll-out decks, which are empty areas along the tops of the walls. Spectators watch from the outer portions of the decks.

● *Slopestyle*

A slopestyle course is filled with obstacles arranged in random order. As riders choose their course, they perform tricks to impress the judges. A **railslide** is a typical obstruction on a slopestyle course. A railslide is a metal or wooden bar or a downed tree. A rider travels on the railslide and launches off it. A quarterpipe, which is a halfpipe with just one wall, is another type of obstacle riders face.

● *Judging*

Freestyle judges sit on a platform at the bottom of the run and have a clear view of the course. At least three, but no more than five, judges score the events. If there are five judges, each competitor's top and bottom scores are thrown out.

Riders perform two runs. The rider with the highest combined score wins the competition. Judges rate the performances on the following scale:

81-100	Excellent
61-80	Above average
41-60	Average
21-40	Below average
0-20	Poor

The judges consider these criteria.

Style: Performance of the program in a smooth and flowing manner.

Aggressiveness: Performance of each maneuver to its limit.

Execution: Precision, stability, balance, and control.

Degree of Difficulty: Difficulty of each maneuver and the entire program.

Originality and Variety: Number of tricks, organization of the program, and use of the pipe and obstacles.

Falls: Each judge assesses a penalty for a fall. The severity of the penalty depends on how the fall affected the overall performance and what maneuver was being attempted when the fall occurred.

Race Competition

● Slalom

The slalom course is designed to allow racers to combine speed with precise execution of turns and skillful use of the terrain. Competitors ride down a vertical drop of between 260 and 500 feet, through a series of gates marked by pairs of poles. Gates alternate red and blue down the run to aid racers in identifying the course.

There are between 30 and 70 gates. The gates are set no closer than 3 feet apart and no farther than 50 feet. The gates are arranged at varying intervals to test the widest variety of downhill techniques, including changes of direction, terrain, and rhythm. Racers take two runs on different courses. The competitor with the fastest combined time wins.

● Parallel Slalom

Two similar courses are arranged side by side for the parallel slalom. Competitors are matched in racing pairs according to bib numbers. Number one races number two, number three races number four, and so on. Racers with odd numbers race on the righthand course for the first run. Racers with even numbers race on the lefthand course for the first run. They switch courses for the second run. The racer with the best combined time wins.

● Giant Slalom

The giant slalom course drops between 300 and 900 feet, presenting riders with a variety of wide and medium turns. Racers in this high-speed event find their own line between the gates.

A giant slalom gate consists of two poles on either side held together by banners. The poles are connected by red, then blue, banners. The distance between the gates is no less than 30 feet, with no maximum distance. Competitors take two runs. For the second run, some gates are placed in different positions. The racer with the fastest combined time is the winner.

● Super G

The super G course requires a variety of wide and medium turns across the full width of the trail. Two poles with connecting banners mark the super G run, which is down a vertical drop between 500 and 1,300 feet. Gates are set no less than 20 feet and no more than 40 feet downslope from each other.

Super G competitors are allowed only one run. With no chance of making up time in a second run, they ride aggressively.

● Special Equipment

To achieve the highest possible speeds, snowboard racers wear formfitting bodysuits. They ride extra-narrow boards for quick turning, and wear hard-shell boots for maximum ankle support around sharp corners. Helmets are mandatory for giant slalom and super G races.

Aggressive racing means smashing through gate poles as much as going around them. Riders in slalom events wear shoulder pads, face masks, reinforced gloves, and shin pads to protect themselves. All competitors wear numbered bibs on their chests and backs to identify themselves.

● Race Rules

A racer correctly passes a gate if he or she has two feet on the board and the entire board crosses the gate line. If a rider misses a gate, he or she must either go back through the gate or im-

mediately leave the course. If a racer isn't sure whether he or she correctly passed a gate, he or she asks the gate judge. If the judge answers "go," the gate was passed. If the judge answers "back," the gate must be repassed. If the gate judge isn't sure, the rider gets credit for the gate.

A competitor may be disqualified from the competition for missing a gate, having an early or delayed start, performing illegal tricks in freestyle events, not passing the finish line with at least one foot fixed on the snowboard, accepting help from someone during a run, or not leaving the course promptly after completing a run.

Chapter 5

PRACTICE, PRACTICE

Snowboarding asks many things of its riders. They must have the strength to push against forces that are sometimes twice their body weight or more. They must have the endurance to withstand bone-crunching landings and muscle-burning turns. To strap on a board at the top of a steep slope demands courage.

But the most important quality a rider must have is determination. A determined beginner can, by day's end, glide down an entire mountain without falling. Endurance, courage, and strength are acquired along the way. Without determination, the strongest and bravest athlete may give up in an hour.

Beginning snowboarders fall as often as babies learning to walk. Having both feet tied onto a board is a very strange

sensation. If you're used to skateboarding, you will feel especially frustrated when you're losing your balance and can't get a foot loose to catch yourself. Fortunately, most people will begin to feel at ease and under control after one or two days of effort.

The rewards of perseverance are many. Snowboarding is great exercise. A full day on the slopes equals any workout in a gym or weight room. Snowboarding conditions the entire body from the heart and lungs to the muscles of the stomach, legs, and even the arms.

Conditioning

It's wise to come to the mountain prepared for the challenge. While riding often is the best way to maintain snowboarding fitness, off-snow training can also be very effective. Janine has come to Mount Hood to work on her skills at summer snowboard camp. Before going up the mountain she stretches to loosen the muscles of her legs, arms, back, and neck. Stretching is the key to injury prevention and should be done before any workout.

Janine feels confident of her snowboarding fitness because she has conditioned herself at home. Since all snowboarding turns are performed by resisting the forces of momentum and gravity, her off-snow workouts always include strengthening exercises. First, Janine demonstrates wall-sits. She leans her back and head against a wall and sits as if there were a chair beneath her. She times herself for one minute and then takes a one-minute rest before doing it again.

Next Janine takes an easy hike up a nearby hill. On the way down, she takes long reaching strides. Her goal is to keep her speed under control, not to see how fast she can go. She repeats this three or four times. Resistance exercises such as wall-sits and downhill running condition the leg muscles that are in heavy demand while riding. Sit-ups, weight lifting, and chin-ups can also help, especially when the downward motion is performed slowly.

Janine also does aerobic activities that help her lungs, upper body, and heart work more efficiently. Bicycling, swimming, jogging, and rope jumping are some of Janine's favorites.

Sports such as waterskiing, surfing, skateboarding, wakeboarding, wind-surfing, and gymnastics events like the balance beam and trampoline also help you develop balance, body control, and flexibility. These skills transfer directly to snowboarding.

Ways to Practice

Taking basic skills and combining them into a series of movements is the most effective way to gain confidence and proficiency on the snowboard. The three drills that follow will help you improve your ability to turn, slow down, speed up, and stop.

● *Downhill to Sideslip to Downhill*

Trevor feels confident going down the hill sideways. Now he wants to ride forward but still maintain his control. To do this, he alternates between sideways and forward riding.

He begins on an easy run. He's in the sideslip position. When he is ready to ride forward, he shifts his weight onto his front foot. This frees his back foot to kick the snowboard uphill. Now some of his weight is redistributed onto his back foot, while most of it remains forward to keep the front of the board going straight. When Trevor wants to slow down, he shifts his weight onto his front foot, kicks his rear foot downhill, and digs his toe edge into the snow. He continues downhill by again shifting his weight forward.

● *Traverse to Skid Turn to Traverse*

On a wide, uncrowded slope, Trevor cuts a shallow path across the run by rooting himself firmly over his toe edge. At the run's boundary, he twists his upper body at the waist and focuses his eyes on a spot 180 degrees behind him.

Trevor shifts his weight onto his front foot and kicks his rear foot until his heel edge catches the snow on the up-hill side. Next, he redistributes his weight evenly on both legs and balances himself firmly over his heel edge.

● *Downhill to Skid to Stop*

Amy can ride forward but she has difficulty stopping without falling. To correct this, she takes the stop in easy steps.

She begins by riding downhill. As her speed increases, she shifts some of her weight over the nose of her board. She gradually slides her back foot downhill while increasing the pressure on her toe edge.

As Amy turns sideways to the slope, she redistributes her weight evenly onto both legs and leans uphill in a skid. As she slows, she leans gradually over the top of the board until she comes to a complete stop.

Chapter 6

STUNTS

There are many outstanding snow-boarders, but no one has ever mas-tered every technique. Original stunts are being invented every day. Snow-boarders are constantly learning new skills and refining old ones. To see a talented rider leap and twist and grace-fully alight upon the snow is like watch-ing a remarkable ballet as it is being created. On a snowboard, there is al-ways something more to learn.

Fakie

As soon as new riders master the basic maneuvers, most are eager to try the more difficult moves of freestyle snow-boarding. One skill is essential to freestyle snowboarding: the ability to ride backward. This is known as riding **fakie,** or in a **switch-stance.** Excellent snowboarders ride equally well no mat-ter which foot is in the lead. They switch effortlessly on the fly—left foot first, then right one.

Learning to ride fakie is, for many people, like learning to ride all over again. The quickest way to learn to ride

Super Snowboarder

When Craig Kelly retired from professional snowboard competition in 1991, he had won four world championships (1986–1989) and three overall U.S. titles (1987–1989). Craig, who has a degree in chemical engineering from the University of Washington, still rides and promotes snowboarding.

He was born on April 1, 1966, and grew up in Mount Vernon, Washington, in the shadow of towering Mount Baker (11,000 feet). As a child, Craig dreamed of playing professional baseball. He didn't go skiing until he was 15, and then, he only went twice. Later that same year, he went to Mount Baker a third time and tried snowboarding with his friend, Jeff Fulton. Craig instantly loved snowboarding. He and his friends rode at every chance. They encour-aged each other to create new moves.

Craig finished fourth in his first contest, at Mount Baker in 1984. Just two years later, however, Craig won the World Slalom Championship at Breckenridge, Colorado. It was his first major victory.

fakie is to devote entire days to riding with your rear foot in front. This method takes about as much time and effort as learning to ride in the first place. You will take your lumps again, so do this only when soft snow covers the mountain.

A more gradual way to learn to ride fakie is to practice the **alternating traverse**. In this drill, Trevor draws a falling-leaf pattern in the snow while sliding side to side down the hill. Rather than making turns, Trevor switches lead feet by alternating his weight from right to left. Whichever foot is first bears the majority of Trevor's weight. When Trevor is ready to change direction, he simply bends the knee of his front leg and straightens his back leg.

Meet Michele Taggert

Born: *May 6, 1970*

Home: *Salem, Oregon*

How she started snowboarding: *After watching her big brother ride for a couple of years, Michele worked up the courage to try herself. She entered the halfpipe contest at the Hoodoo Ski Bowl in Oregon her third time on a snowboard. "I loved catching airs," Michelle said. "I just threw myself up the walls and launched as high as I could. Then I'd crash back down in the pipe and do it again. The judges liked my aggressiveness and I won!"*

Turning Pro: *At the age of 18, one and a half years after she began riding, Michelle became a professional.*

Top Career Honor: *She won the1993–94 World All-Around Championship at Ishgal, Austria. "I had to compete in the halfpipe, slalom, and giant slalom," Michelle said. "It was my goal to become world champion, but I hadn't planned on it happening so soon. I was really surprised. It was really cool."*

Advice to beginning riders: *"Don't give up after one or two times. At first it's frustrating, but after that, just have a good time. You'll learn so quick if you stick with it, you can't help but have a good time."*

Railslide

A railslide is a bar, similar to a handrail along a staircase, or a downed tree. When sliding on a tree, be sure it's dead because otherwise it soon will be. A snowboarder rides over the railslide and launches off it. The simplest railslides to master are those which rise from ground level. Snowboarders call sliding down anything that isn't snow **jibbing** or bonking.

Dylan uses a skid while approaching the rail to control his speed and get lined up. Once on the rail, Dylan assumes a normal riding stance and enjoys the trip. As his feet come to the upper lip of the railslide, Dylan twists at the waist and pushes off with his legs.

In the air, Dylan's snowboard follows in the direction of his twist. Dylan stops the turn by focusing on the point on which he wants to land. He lets the rear of his snowboard touch the snow first to avoid a face-first fall.

Falling off a railslide can hurt. Practice this maneuver only after a heavy snow and first check for hidden obstructions.

Launch

Cliffs, boulders, downed trees—anything that causes the snowboarder to become airborne—is a launch. Catching air can be the biggest thrill of your life. It can also be the biggest disaster. Before departing over the lip of a cliff, ride across the landing area two or three times and check for rocks, trees, or other snow-covered obstructions. Failure to ensure a safe landing area could result in serious injury or even death. It's always a good idea to consult an experienced local rider before taking flight into unknown airspace.

After clearing the landing area, you're ready to fly. As you near the top of the launch, curb your speed with a series of turns. The best way to ensure a good landing is to make a good approach. Prepare to leave the ground by getting as low as possible. Bend at your knees and hips.

While in the air, grab your snowboard to keep your body under control. Like an airplane lowering its landing gear, open your stance and feel for the ground with the rear end of your snowboard. Landing tail first prevents the nose of the board from digging into the snow and throwing the rider into a wild cartwheel. Complete the flight by sinking gracefully onto the mountain and resuming your normal riding posture.

Powder and Back Country

For snowboarders, there is no such thing as too much snow. Like a surfboard on a wave, snowboards glide on powder that may be over the rider's head. Riding on deep powder can feel like floating—provided the snow is fresh and light.

To ride deep powder, it's necessary to have a steep slope. Without speed, there's simply no way to stay on top of the snow. The best steep, powdery slopes are often found in the back country, away from the heavily trampled runs of ski resorts. Whenever you're riding in the back country, make

Snowboard Parks

Many ski resorts have a special section of the slopes set aside where riders meet, practice tricks, and learn from each other. Snowboard parks featuring halfpipes, quarterpipes, jumps, platforms, railslides, and slalom courses began popping up in the early 1990s. At that time, many areas began to attract as many snowboarders as skiers. To attract even greater numbers of riders, ski areas constructed parks.

Many parks have "snowboarders only" tow-ropes so that riders can get up the hill quickly and practice a trick many times a day. The snowboard parks helped create a surge of interest in places generally considered flatland. Thanks to these parks, you are as likely to find a great halfpipe rider in Minnesota as you are in Colorado.

sure you ride with a partner. Let some-one else know where you're going. Also, check with park rangers or the ski patrol about the possible danger of avalanches.

To stay on top of the snow, you must lean heavily on your rear foot. This keeps the nose of your board above the powder, preventing it from sinking in. Because your rear leg will tire quickly with so much weight on it, turn often.

As on shallower runs, you still have to shift your weight forward whenever you change direction. This will give your rear leg a moment of rest and make it possi-ble for you to carve the slope without stopping. In extremely deep snow, try to avoid stopping because getting started again may be difficult.

One place that almost always has great snow, even at busy resorts, is in the trees. Trees provide a natural slalom course. Snowboarding through the trees can be an exciting and satis-fying experience.

Before entering unfamiliar woods, find out from a knowledgeable local

rider where you will finish. It's no fun to discover a deep river full of cold water that must be crossed to get home. Always ride with a partner. Also, when riding out of bounds at ski areas or in remote locations, let someone know where you're going. Think ahead. Plan two or three moves in advance to be sure you always have a way out, and wear goggles to protect your eyes from branches.

Snowboarding is a young sport that is changing as quickly as it's growing. No matter what your reasons are for strapping on a board, you will help shape this amazing pastime.

SNOWBOARDING TALK

alpine: A style of snowboard designed for flowing curves and high speeds.

alternating traverse: A drill in which the snowboarder draws a falling-leaf pattern with the snowboard as he or she goes down the slope. Used when learning to ride fakie.

asymmetrical: Not the same on both sides. An asymmetrical snowboard is designed for speed and ease in alpine-style carving turns.

backside: Maneuvers that are done on the heelside edge when the rider is facing downhill.

binding: A device that holds a rider's foot to a snowboard.

carve: To turn sharply on the snowboard's edge without sliding. A carved turn leaves a thin track in the snow.

catching air: To become airborne or take flight on a snowboard.

fakie: To ride down the hill with the snowboarder's rear foot going first. Also called **switch-stance.**

flex: The flexibility of a snowboard. A stiffer, less flexible board may be easier to ride on ice, hard snow, or deep powder. A softer, more flexible board is recommended for softer surfaces.

freestyle: A competitive event in which riders do a variety of moves using railslides, bumps, halfpipes, and other tricks.

frontside: Maneuvers that are done on the toeside edge when the rider is facing uphill.

giant slalom: A competitive event in which riders race down a course with gates. The racers choose their own paths through the widely dispersed gates.

goofy: A riding stance in which the snowboarder's right foot is forward.

halfpipe: A rounded channel dug out of the snow. Riders use the side walls as launches for catching air and performing tricks.

hardpack: Snow that has been compressed into ice or become choppy and hard.

International Snowboard Federation (ISF): The sanctioning body for professional competitions all over the world.

jibbing: Hitting the snowboard on something other than snow, such as a barrel or a rail. Also called bonking.

launch: A cliff or other formation used by snowboarders to become airborne.

leash: A rope or band attached to the front binding and fastened around a snowboarder's leg to prevent runaway snowboards.

parallel slalom: A competitive race in which two snowboarders ride identical side-by-side courses at the same time.

powder: Soft, fresh snow.

railslide: A wooden or metal rail or a downed tree that snowboarders slide on and use to become airborne.

regular: A riding stance in which the snowboarder's left foot is in the lead.

shovel: The rounded, upturned tip of the snowboard.

sideslip: To go down a run with the snowboard sideways on the slope.

skating: A pushing motion, similar to skateboarding, that snowboarders use on flat surfaces.

skid: A maneuver in which the snowboarder puts more weight on the uphill edge to control his or her speed without stopping or turning.

slalom: A competitive race in which riders race against time through a course of gates.

slopestyle: A competitive freestyle event in which snowboarders do tricks off launches and obstacles.

stomp pad: The pad installed on a snowboard to provide friction when the snowboarder's foot is riding out of the rear binding.

super G: A competitive race event in which snowboarders do a variety of medium and long turns across the entire slope. An abbreviation of super giant slalom.

switch-stance: A riding technique in which the snowboarder goes down the hill with his or her rear foot in the lead. Also called riding **fakie.**

traverse: To move back and forth across the slope.

United States Amateur Snowboard Association (USASA): The sanctioning body for amateur competitions in the United States.

FOR MORE INFORMATION

Alpine Surf Wear
605 Bank Street
Wallace, ID 83873

Bored Magazine
364 North 77th Street
Seattle, WA 98103

Burton Snowboards
P. O. Box 4449
Burlington, VT 05406-4449

Gnu, Lib-tech Snowboards
2600 West Commodore Way
Seattle, WA 98199

International Snowboard Federation
P. O. Box 477
Vail, CO 81658

National Snowboard Inc.
P. O. Box 1168
Conifer, CO 80433

Snowboard Educators of North
America
4352 Onyx Point
Eagan, MN 55122

Snowboard Magazine
2814 Fairfield Avenue, Suite 137
Bridgeport, CT 06605

Snowboarder Magazine
P. O. Box 1028
Dana Point, CA 92629

TransWorld SNOWboarding Magazine
353 Airport Road
Oceanside, CA 92054

United States Amateur Snowboard
Association (USASA)
c/o Chuck Allen
P. O. Box 8251
Green Valley Lake, CA 92341

United States Snowboarding Team
1500 Kearns Boulevard
P. O. Box 100
Park City, UT 84060

FURTHER READING

Althen, K.C. *The Complete Book of Snowboarding.* Rutland, Vt.: Charles E. Tuttle Company, Inc., 1990.

Garcia, Elena. *A Beginner's Guide to Zen and the Art of Snowboarding.* Berkeley, Calif.: Amberco Press, 1990.

McMullen, John. *The Basic Essentials of Snowboarding.* Merrillville, Ind.: ICS Books, Inc., 1991.

Reichenfeld, Rob, and Anna Bruechert. *Snowboarding.* Champaign, Ill.: Human Kinetics Publishers, Inc., 1995.

INDEX